The Work Of Mentall Illness is **God's +**

A Journey with Mental Illness: A True
Story by Rev. Dr. Holistic Life Coach
Tyrone Waters

The Work Of Mentall Illness is

God's +

A Journey with Mental Illness: A True
Story by Rev. Dr. Holistic Life Coach
Tyrone Waters

DR. TYRONE WATERS

ARPress
ILLUMINATING IDEAS
EMPOWERING VOICES

ARPress
45 Dan Road Suite 5
Canton MA 02021

Hotline:1(888) 821-0229
Fax:1(508) 545-7580

Ordering Information:
Quantity sales. Special discounts are available
on quantity purchases by corporations,
associations, and others. For details, contact
the publisher at the address above.

Printed in the United States of America.

ISBN-13:

Paperback   979-8-89356-895-0
eBook   979-8-89356-894-3

Library of Congress Control Number:
2024904708

LAWMAKER'S SON LEAVES JAIL FOR PSYCHIATRIC- Oregonian, The (Portland, OR)- May 10, 2002- page C09

May 10, 2002| Oregonian, The (Portland, OR)| MICHELLE ROBERTS – The Oregonian| Page C09

Summary: Tyrone Wayne Waters, son of state Sen. Avel Gordly, faces charges in a gun case.

The mentally ill son of state Sen. Avel Gordly was transferred from a jail isolation cell to a Portland psychiatric hospital on Monday on a judge's order.

Multnomah County Circuit Judge Julie E. Frants signed the order late Wednesday to commit Gordly's son, Tyrone Wayne Waters, 36, to the Oregon State Hospital in Portland, 1225 N.E. Second Avenue.

Although Frantz agreed last week that Waters was not mentally competent to participate in his defense against an attempted aggravated murder charge, a dilemma remained about where to place him.

Frantz was forced to consider alternatives to jail and the Oregon State Hospital, which is under investigation into its treatment of Waters.

Waters was arrested on Sept. 17 after he allegedly aimed a pellet gun at Portland police outside a home on North Williams Avenue during a psychotic episode. Gordly, who was concerned about her son's mental state, had called police to the home.

Officers fired five live rounds and two beanbag rounds, striking Waters with a beanbag round.

All parties to the case agreed that

Waters could not be sent back to the state hospital in Salem. The Oregon Department of Justice is investigating allegations that hospital employees made racist comments about Waters while he was a patient there from Oct. 5 until March 21. The investigation is expected to be done by mid-month.

"The court recommends the defendant be placed at the Portland facility due to the unique circumstances of this case," Frantz wrote in her order.

Since March 21, Waters has been held in the Multnomah County Detention Center after a state hospital doctor changed his diagnosis from paranoid schizophrenia to paranoid personality disorder, a behavioral problem, and deemed him mentally capable of standing trial. The investigation is also looking into the timing of the change in his diagnosis.

For the past three weeks, Waters has

been in an isolation jail cell, on so-called "lockdown," because of his behavior. He refused medication and had no access to county mental health staff, his mother said.

Waters will be held at the secure hospital until Frantz rules he can effectively assist his lawyer in the defense of his case.

TREAT HIM AS A CRIMINAL- Oregonian, The (Portland, OR)- June 11, 2002- page B08

June 11, 2002 | Oregonian, The (Portland, OR) | Page B08

Regarding the articles pertaining to state Sen. Avel Gordly's son, Tyrone Waters (June 2–3), Gordly, as a mother, would like to act as judge and jury by having her son treated for a mental illness instead of being incarcerated by the criminal justice system for waving or pointing a weapon at a police officer.

This mother requested an African American police commander when her son reeled out of control, and she wanted her son evaluated and treated by a mental health professional of similar ethnic and cultural background.

Mental illness can be found regardless of gender, ethnicity, and socioeconomic level. Waters indicated he was comfortable with his first psychiatrist, who was white. It was Waters who chose to end treatment and cease taking medication.

I can't imagine asking race or gender questions when making a doctor's appointment. Insurance regulations would render such options impossible. Pointing or waving a weapon at an officer is a crime.

Our applause goes out to the Oregonian's reporter, Michelle Roberts, and to Sen. Avel Gordly, D-Portland, who together told a touching story long overdue in Oregon.

The series "When race and mental illness collide" (June 2–3) uncovered the sad truth behind the treatment of Gordly's son, Tyrone Waters, who suffers from mental illness.

Waters is just one of many African Americans in Oregon who receive unfair treatment. As the president of the African American Health Coalition and as an advocate on the State Mental Health Advisory Committee, I know firsthand that discrimination against African Americans in the mental health system is a reality.

As the article stated, the prevalence of mental disorders is estimated to be higher among African Americans than whites because of stressors such as poverty and discrimination. Yet because of the mistrust that African Americans are feeling and because of stigma, cost, and some clinician bias, it is much more difficult for them to receive appropriate treatment.

African American men and women are admitted to psychiatric hospitals more than two times as often as whites.

I am not suggesting criminals go unpunished. I am only suggesting we get them the treatment they need so that there are fewer Tyrone Waters in jail and more people like him getting the help they need to live safe and productive lives in Rose City.

Summary: The Oregon State Hospital technician who disparaged Tyrone Wayne Waters no longer works at the facility

Investigators have determined that an African American psychiatric patient who is the son of State Sen. Avel Gordly was verbally abused two months ago during his stay at the Oregon State Hospital in Portland.

The Office of Investigations and Training found that on May 1, an EKG technician working in the psychiatric ward made disparaging remarks to Tyrone Wayne Waters, 36.

In a report dated July 19, hospital superintendent Stanley Mazur-Hart determined that the employee called Waters a "smart ass." When Waters asked the employee his name, the employee responded that it was "Billy Bob."

"Multiple staff present at the time of the event corroborated (Waters') statement, "Mazur-Hart wrote in the report, adding that the staff member "could not be located and was no longer employed by the contracting agency."

The finding comes a month after the attorney general's office concluded that Oregon State Hospital should provide employees with in-depth and ongoing cultural training after a much broader investigation found that "inappropriate" racial conversations had taken place inside the state's largest psychiatric facility in Salem.

The Department of Human Services concluded its own review in May, and Mazur-Hart determined that, even though employees had made insensitive statements, Waters and others hadn't heard them and therefore hadn't been harmed.

Waters, who was diagnosed with paranoid schizophrenia by the hospital in the mid-1990s, was a patient from Oct. 5, 2001, until March 21, when a state hospital doctor deemed him mentally capable to stand trial. A judge, however, ordered him back to the hospital, this time in Portland, where another doctor has since found him unable to aid and assist.

Waters was arrested on Sept. 17 after he allegedly aimed a pellet gun at Portland police during a psychotic break, according to police and medical records. He is accused of attempted aggravated murder, charges that may or may not stand when a grand jury ultimately considers Waters' mental condition and the fact that he held a pellet gun.

Reached Tuesday, Waters said he is relieved that the most recent allegation of abuse was corroborated. "I feel so much better that people are listening to what's happening here. It makes me less afraid to be here. I'm still afraid. But less afraid."

The death threat to the governor should not have led to the Oregonian, The (Portland, OR) May 11, 2018 (page 13).

A man committed to psychiatric care for six months after he threatened to kill Gov. Kate Brown didn't meet the legal threshold for being held and treated against his will, the Oregon Court of Appeals ruled Wednesday.

In June 2015, Tyrone Waters left

an expletive-laden voicemail with Brown's office repeatedly stating that he planned to "kill" Brown or that she was "dead" because she was his "enemy.".

Although the Appeals Court described the voicemail as "highly disturbing," judges ruled there was no evidence that Waters, who was living in San Diego at the time, had actual plans to follow through on his threats.

Other concerning behavior—including that Waters thought he was a bounty hunter and he carried handcuffs and pepper spray—didn't prove he was "highly likely" to harm himself or others, which is the legal standard for civil commitments in Oregon, the Appeals Court ruled.

The court said it had no evidence to show Waters had used the handcuffs or pepper spray to take anyone into custody.

The court found that Multnomah County Circuit Judge Pro Tem Elizabeth Fithian-Barrett erred in committing Waters in September 2015.

Waters, who was 49 then, is the son of former state Sen. Avel Gordly, who has spoken publicly of his struggles. Her advocacy for all people with mental illness prompted Oregon Health & Science University in 2008 to rename its behavioral health unit the Avel Gordly Center for Healing.

Neither Waters nor Gordly could reach her comment.

Water's battles with mental illness began in his 20s, when he was diagnosed with schizophrenia. In 2001, he was sent to a Portland psychiatric hospital after he hallucinated and pointed a pellet gun at police officers in front of his grandfather's home in North Portland, according to the

Appeals Court summary.

Waters stabilized on medication and did well for years after that, the court stated. He worked as a peer counselor for Cascadia Behavioral Health, but then switched medications and became consumed with fear about living in the United States as a gay, African American man, the court summary said.

He worried that others would hurt or kill him and unsuccessfully sought asylum in Canada in 2015, the summary states.

Months later, he left a hostile voicemail with the governor's office.

Waters' successful appeal for his civil commitment is somewhat of a hollow victory. He was committed to psychiatric care for up to 180 days in 2015, and that term has long passed.

But the ruling once again established the high bar that Oregon appellate courts have set for committing people with mental illness against their will.

The decision was made by a three-judge panel of the Appeals Court. Judges Joel DeVore and Roger DeHoog ruled for the majority. Judge Erin Lagesen dissented, saying it was "highly likely" that Waters was a danger to himself and others, given the evidence in the case.

CONFRONTATION ENDS WITH MAN IN CUSTODY- Oregonian, The (Portland, OR)- September 21, 2001- page D03

September 21, 2001 | Oregonian, The (Portland, OR)| MAXINE BERNSTEIN- The Oregonian | Page 003

Summary: A man threatening officers with a pellet gun is held for mental health evaluation, then placed in jail

A Portland man with a mental illness who had taped threats against police on his phone's answering machine is accused of attempted aggravated murder after he pointed a pellet gun at officers who were called to his home Monday night, police said.

An officer-safety alert was distributed to Portland officers last week about threats that Tyrone Wayne Waters, 35, of the 4500 block of North Williams Avenue had made against the police.

On his answering machine message, Waters spoke angrily of his Sept. 1 arrest at the Jantzen Beach Center mall after a confrontation on a Tri-Met bus.

The bus driver radioed Tri-Met dispatch that Waters had threatened another passenger with what looked like a real gun. Police found Waters at the mall carrying a BB gun in his briefcase. They seized the BB gun and accused Waters of unlawful possession of a firearm. He was to appear in court on Sept. 26.

On the recording, Waters vowed not to come to court but instead pledged to seek "vigilante justice," warning that there would be a "shootout" between him and the police that day and that he wanted the officers "dead."

On Monday night, family members who were concerned about Waters' mental state contacted Northeast

Precinct Cmdr. Derrick Foxworth. Waters is the son of state Sen. **Avel Gordly**, D-Portland.

Foxworth and Sgt. Kevin Modica went to the home at 6:51 p.m. and talked to a family member outside. Waters, who was sitting on the front porch, walked toward the officers, Foxworth said.

"We yelled out to him, 'Tyrone, we're just here to check with you. How are you doing? ' "Foxworth said. Foxworth said Waters froze, pulled a gun from his backpack, and raised it.

According to Foxworth and police and court reports, the officers ordered Waters to drop the gun and called for cover officers. Officer Kevin Felts fired two beanbag rounds and struck Waters, who continued to hold his gun.

Officer Doug Matthews fired five live

rounds at Waters that did not hit him. Waters dropped to the ground and was taken by ambulance to Legacy Emanuel Hospital & Health Center for a mental health evaluation. The gun he was carrying was a pellet gun.

Sgt. Brian Schmautz, Portland Police Bureau spokesman, said Waters was to have been placed on a 72-hour mental health hold, but he was released back to police after 24 hours and jailed. A hospital spokeswoman said Legacy Emanuel could not comment about the case.

Gordly criticized the jailing of her son and said the lack of mental health beds is a statewide crisis that has affected her son.

"My son is not a criminal. He has a mental illness. What is criminal is the fact that there are no mental health beds available anywhere in the state," Gordly said.

"We should all be ashamed of that fact and do everything in our power to correct the problem. Jail is not the place to be providing treatment to those with the misfortune of having a brain disorder."

A Multnomah County grand jury will hear the case against Waters next week. Felts and Matthews were placed on routine administrative leave after firing at Waters.

PATIENT ENTERS TRANSTIONAL PROGRAM- CHARGES ARE- OREGONIAN, THE (PORTLAND, OR)- September 10, 2002—page B01

September 10, 2002| Oregonian, The (Portland, OR)| MICHELLE ROBERTS- The Oregonian |Page B01

Summary: Tyrone Waters, whose treatment sparked an inquiry into racism, is released with conditions

Tyrone Waters was released from jail Monday, nearly one year after he allegedly aimed a pellet gun at Portland police during a psychotic episode.

Waters, 36, clutching a brown grocery bag of psychiatric medication, walked out of the Multnomah County Justice Center jail in downtown Portland hours after a judge determined he was no longer a danger to himself or others.

Waters, the son of State Sen. Avel Gordly, remains charged on the prosecutor's information with attempted aggravation in the confrontation with police on Sept. 17, 2001. However, Waters' psychiatric condition has improved so markedly during the past four months that Multnomah County Circuit Judge Julie Frantz released him pending resolution of the criminal case.

"I'm looking forward to getting on with my life," Waters said. "I feel really confident that, with the help of my case manager, I will be able to follow all the conditions the court has placed on me. I'm so thankful for this opportunity."

Prosecutors did not object to the release of Waters, who will stay at the Bridgeview Community in downtown Portland, a transitional housing program that helps people with serious mental illnesses prepare for independent living.

"As of right now, the community is safe, and he's safe," said John Bradley, Multnomah County's first assistant district attorney. "As long as he's willing to take his medication."

Conditions of release

Taking his medication without fail, following the rules at Bridgeview, and being under close street supervision were among the many conditions of Water's release.

A settlement conference to resolve the criminal charges against him will be held in three weeks after Waters receives another psychiatric evaluation, and there has been time to gauge his progress in the community, said Randall Vogt, Waters' attorney.

One settlement proposal discussed in court Monday would require Waters to plead guilty, but for insanity, to a Class C felony, Vogt said. Waters would be monitored by the Psychiatric Security Review Board for five years, and he would be required to take his psychiatric medications or return to the Oregon State Hospital in Salem.

Shortly after his arrest last September, Frantz sent Waters to the state hospital, where he was to receive treatment to restore his fitness for trial or to make other decisions about his case. The same hospital had diagnosed Waters with paranoid schizophrenia in the mid-1990s.

During his treatment, allegations that hospital employees had made racist comments about Waters drew the attention of the highest levels of state government and sparked an investigation into minority patients' treatment at Oregon's largest psychiatric hospital.

Training recommended

The inquiry by the Oregon Department of Justice eventually concluded that, even though employees had made insensitive statements, Waters and others hadn't heard them and therefore hadn't been harmed. Even so, the team recommended that the hospital require cultural competency training for all workers.

On March 21, 10 days after the investigation began, a hospital psychiatrist declared Waters able to aid and assist in his defense and changed his diagnosis from paranoid schizophrenia to paranoid personality disorder, a behavioral problem, records show.

Waters was taken back to the Justice Center jail to face charges, even though he remained psychotic and paranoid. After her own observation of Waters in court hearings—during which he screamed, spat at a prosecutor, and announced he was hearing voices—Judge Frantz went against the state hospital recommendation and declared Waters unable to aid and assist.

SENATOR'S FIGHT FOR SON HITS NEEDS OF MENTALLY ILL- Oregonian, The (Portland, OR)- April 30, 2002- page B01

April 30, 2002 | Oregonian, The (Portland, OR) | MAXINE BERNSTEIN – The Oregonian | Page B01

Summary: Avel Gordly argues that her son is not competent to stand trial on an attempted murder charge and needs care, not a jail cell

State Sen. Avel Gordly told a Multnomah County judge Monday that her son is not mentally competent to stand trial in a pending criminal case and called his current isolation in jail inhumane.

"My son is not a criminal. "Gordly, D-Portland testified in an emotional hearing before Judge Julie E. Frantz that ended with her son being forced from the courtroom after he spat on a district attorney. "He needs to be and deserves to be in a treatment center."

Although Frantz agreed Monday that Gordly's son, Tyrone Wayne Waters, 36, was not mentally competent to participate in his defense against an attempted aggravated murder charge, a dilemma remains about where to place him.

A hearing is scheduled for Friday to consider alternatives to jail and the Oregon State Hospital, which is under investigation into its treatment of Waters.

Gordly said her son's case highlights the inadequacies of the county's and state's mental health systems and that she is tired of officials blaming a lack of money or resources. She called on the court to find better ways to support her son and others in the criminal justice system who suffer from mental illnesses.

"What this has got to do is force the county and the state to deal with this issue, "said Gordly, who was surrounded by dozens of relatives, friends, and church members. "Because we can't find a hospital bed or a county community resource, he has to stay in jail? What we're doing is inhumane."

Waters was arrested Sept. 17 after he allegedly aimed a pellet gun at Portland police outside a home on North Williams Avenue during a psychotic episode, according to the police and medical records.

Family members who were concerned about Water's mental state had called police to the home. Officers fired five live rounds and two beanbag rounds, striking Waters with a beanbag round.

All parties to the case agree that Waters cannot be sent back to the state hospital. The Oregon Department of

Justice is investigating allegations that hospital employees made racist comments about Waters while he was a patient there from Oct. 5 until March 21. The investigation is expected to be done by mid-May, said Pam Curtis, a health care policy analyst in the governor's office.

Since March 21, Waters has been held in the Multnomah County Detention Center after a state hospital doctor changed his diagnosis from paranoid schizophrenia to paranoid personality disorder, a behavioral problem, and deemed him mentally capable of standing trial. The investigation is also looking into the timing of the change in his diagnosis.

For the past two weeks, Waters has been in an isolation jail cell, so-ccalled "lockdown," because of his behavior. He has refused medication and has had no access to county mental health staff, his mother said.

"He's in lockup because he's acting out—behaviors that come out of his illness, "Godly testified. "Treating those behaviors by locking him down does not make sense. I cannot see how conducive that is to getting better. It's an inhumane approach to treating the mentally ill."

On Monday, Frantz reviewed a mental health evaluation of Waters by a second forensic psychologist, Dr. Richard Kolbel, who met with Waters on April 16 and 19 for a total of 5 ½ hours. In his nine-page report, Kolbel found Waters able to aid in his defense, yet he noted that Waters has behavioral swings stemming from mental illness and that his thinking might be delusional.

Waters, wearing a full white jumpsuit with "JAIL" stamped on the back and his right hand cuffed to a metal chain around his waist, stood to address the judge for about 15 minutes. Articulate, coherent, and quoting from case law, Waters complained of mistreatment in jail by the sheriff's deputies and berated the prosecutor, James Mcintyre, and his lawyer, Randall Vogt, for not taking his grievances seriously.

But as the hearing continued, Waters grew agitated, and his voice grew louder. He demanded a new attorney and yelled out when the judge **ruled** that he was unable to participate in his defense, partly due to delusional thinking. "Based on what? "Waters shouted. "Give me an example! "

Frantz scheduled Friday's hearing to address the question of alternative treatment options. Prosecutors, police, Gordly, and county mental health representatives met on April 2 during a meeting called by Northeast Precinct Cmdr. Derrick Foxworth but had no success.

Just as Monday's hearing was ending, Waters stood behind the defense desk, both hands handcuffed to his waist, with two sheriff's deputies standing behind him. As his mother walked up from the gallery to try to speak with her son before he was led away, Waters turned his back to her and walked over to the prosecutor's table.

With a mouthful of saliva, he spat on McIntyre's left side and arm. McIntyre kept his composure and quickly walked into the judge's chambers. Three deputies grabbed Waters' arms and dragged him from the courtroom as onlookers sat stunned. Friends grasped Gordly's hand; some cried.

"There are not adequate options available for the placement of people such as Tyrone," Frantz told Gordly.

"It is an issue Multnomah County must address. Unfortunately, I don't have answers for you. I wish I did."

This city can't keep hiding the mentally ill or putting them in jail. There are too many of them. One in five is the most commonly used statistic. So the next time you want to categorize "those people," start the count with yourself.

S. Renee Mitchell: 503-221-8142; rmitch@news.oregonian.com

HELP THEM- Oregonian, The (Portland, OR)- July 26, 2006- page B01

July 26, 2006 |Oregonian, The (Portland, OR) | S. Renee Mitchell | Page B01

Tyrone Waters wants you to know his story before you judge him.

He was diagnosed with paranoid schizophrenia in his 20s. He has spent time in a Multnomah County jail and in the state mental hospital. And in 2001, he was shot at by Portland police for pointing a pellet gun during a psychotic episode.

Now 40, Waters—son of Sen. Avel Gordly—is medicated, stable, and getting paid to help others with mental illness get their lives back on track.

"We have to remove the stigma that exists in our community, "Waters said at a recent meeting in Northeast Portland. "Sometimes, we don't make the best decisions. But we're able to do that more, and in a better way, with medication and treatment."

As far as he has come, though, Waters is still labeled as one of "those people" that some residents in the Elliot neighborhood don't want to see.

Water's employer, Cascadia Behavioral Healthcare, intends to relocate an outpatient clinic and administrative offices into a block-long vacant building on Northeast Martin Luther King Jr. Boulevard.

But a small and committed number of Elliot residents have been working hard to prevent the inevitable. They feel blindsided by Cascadia's plans to eventually build housing on the site.

"What you want to do is come in and be a part of the community," says Willie Brown, interim director of the Northeast Coalition of

Neighborhoods, which includes Eliot. "They agree that that needs to happen more. But it's kind of like the horse is out of the barn, now."

For years, the coalition has tried—unsuccessfully—to convince the city to put a moratorium on social-service agencies locating clinics, medical buildings, and transitional housing in Northeast Portland.

"It just makes us a neighborhood of special-needs facilities," says Matt Gilley, an Eliot neighborhood association board member.

Some neighborhood leaders tried to encourage developers to buy the Youth Opportunity Center building from Cascadia. They passed out fliers, knocked on doors, and even considered organizing picket lines. They also revived a group called Friends of MLK that purports to advocate for the boulevard's economic health.

Cascadia employees did their own neighborhood polling about a month ago. Of the 15 houses the agency's chief executive officer, Leslie Ford, visited, one was skeptical, one was angry, but the rest were supportive.

"It's not the whole neighborhood that's against this, "Ford says. "Unfortunately, this process repeats itself fairly frequently all over the city."

We all know why no neighborhood is putting out the welcome mat for the folks living among us, hidden in plain sight. We don't want to admit that they exist or that they might be our relatives.

Waters was fortunate. Gordly fought hard to get adequate treatment for her son. She and other family members supported him through his highly publicized work. And Gordly continues to work on legislation to call attention to mental health issues.

"Their recovery is not complete," she says, "without community."

But the community and the social-service providers have to cooperate more. So at some point, this city will have to engage in a larger, more thoughtful conversation about how we will serve the mentally ill among us.

In the fall, Judith Mowry, who was hired to mediate talks between Cascadia and Eliot residents, plans to begin that larger citywide conversation with support from Mayor Tom Potter.

"We have to be able to have this dialogue that is respectful of everybody in the community, "Mowry says. "We need to continue to work on these issues and not give up."

ALLEGED RACISM AT STATE HOSPITAL PROMPTS REVIEW – Oregonian, The (Portland, OR)- April 7, 2002- page A01

April 7, 2002 | Oregonian, The (Portland, OR) | MICHELLE ROBERTS- The Oregonian | Page A01

Summary: Officials scrutinize management and treatment after a senator gets a letter about her son's care

The state attorney general's office will review management practices at Oregon State Hospital after employees allegedly made racist comments about an African American psychiatric patient who is the son of Sen. Avel Gordly, The Oregonian has learned.

The inquiry by the Oregon Department of Justice will seek to determine whether management practices have led to racial harassment, discrimination, and other civil rights violations inside the state's largest psychiatric facility, said Pam Curtis, a health care policy analyst in the governor's office.

Gov. John Kitzhaber's office called for the review and investigation of Gordly's request after she received an anonymous letter on March 6 at her Portland home from a person claiming to be a hospital employee.

Eight employees, including a supervisor, have been reassigned during the investigation into the treatment of Tyrone Wayne Waters, 36, and other African American patients at the Salem hospital.

The Oregon Office of Investigations and Training is also looking at whether its investigation spurred a recent change in Water's psychiatric diagnosis, which caused him to be transferred from the hospital back to jail two weeks ago.

Waters, who has been diagnosed with paranoid schizophrenia since 1994, was a patient from October 5, 2001, until March 21, when a state hospital doctor deemed him mentally capable to stand trial. A judge has since ordered an independent review of Water's mental competency.

It is the first time in memory, officials said, that the attorney general's office has been involved in an investigation into alleged violations at the hospital.

"They're taking this very seriously," said Margy Johnson, deputy assistant director for health services in the Department of Human Services. "Our main goal is to protect the safety and therapeutic environment in the hospital."

The letter Gordly received, obtained

by The Oregonian, named a nurse, three mental health technicians, and a unit of directors who allegedly made repeated racist comments about Waters and other African Americans on Ward 48C, a high security forensics unit.

Gordly said she thinks the letter is credible because the author referred to public remarks she made during a statewide conference on diversity.

At the conference, Gordly, D-Portland, introduced a Portland State University professor who had written a dissertation on post-traumatic slave syndrome. That conference, she said, was attended by several employees and managers at the Oregon State Hospital.

The letter said a group of employees "seized on this statement and began a continual and drawn-out joke. They belittled you for making it.

They belittled your son for believing it, and they belittled black people in general, stating that, in effect, black people are always making lame excuses for themselves and crying the blues."

Investigators are also looking into a flier that was allegedly circulated among staff members mocking Waters, saying he suffered from "multi-ethnic post-past disorder."

"They enjoyed plenty of laughs with this mean-spirited, vile composition," said the letter, which also claimed that the unit of directors "knew about this sick, ongoing joke and did not take action."

"I feel this is a grave matter that sickened me, and I think this should be looked into, "the letter continued. "I also suggest that (hospital superintendent) Stan Mazur-Hart not be the one to look into this because the administration here tries to cover up issues that make them look bad."

Reached Friday, Mazur-Hart said: We just need to see what the review presents. If there is any merit to the allegations, then we would need to work on getting those things fixed.

STATE TEAM FINDS FAULTS AT HOSPITAL= Oregonian, The (Portland, OR)- June 15, 2002- page E01

June 15, 2002 | Oregonian, The (Portland, OR) – MICHELLE ROBERTS- The Oregonian | Page E01

Summary: An inquiry into alleged racism at Oregon State Hospital calls for cultural training of staff

The Oregon attorney general's office concluded Friday that the Oregon State Hospital should provide its employees with in-depth and ongoing cultural training after an investigation found that "inappropriate" racial conversations took place inside the state's largest psychiatric facility.

The attorney general created a three-person team in March to review management practices at the Salem hospital after employees were accused of making racist comments about an African American psychiatric patient who is the son of state Sen. Avel Gordly.

The inquiry by the Oregon Department of Justice sought to determine whether management practices led to racial harassment, discrimination, and other civil rights violations, said Pam Curtis, a health care policy analyst in the governor's office.

"The team didn't find intentional or malicious racism, "Curtis said Friday. "What they did find was communication, staff-to-staff, that was inappropriate and should be prohibited. Those kinds of communications happen all over the place. They shouldn't, but they do."

Gov. John Kitzhaber's office called for the review and investigation of Gordly's request after she received an anonymous letter on March 6 at her Portland home from a person claiming to be a hospital employee.

The anonymous letter named a nurse, three mental health technicians, and a unit director, and they said they made repeated racist comments about Tyrone Wayne Waters, 36, and other African Americans on Ward 48C, a high security forensics unit.

Eight employees, including a supervisor, were reassigned during the investigation. They returned to work in mid-May after the Department of Human Services concluded its review, and Hospital Superintendent Stanley Mazur-Hart determined that, even though employees had made insensitive statements, Waters and others hadn't heard them and therefore hadn't been harmed.

The Department of Justice team, assigned to review the DHS investigation, agreed with Mazur-

Hart's ruling that African American patients did not hear the racially insensitive comments. But the team still found problems.

"The hospital and DHS have policies in place, and they have cultural competency as a goal, but they could be doing a better job working to achieve that goal, "Curtis said.

The team recommended that the hospital require cultural competency training for all workers and that it try to achieve a more diverse work force. Mazur-Hart will work with Kitzhaber's affirmative action director.

Reached Friday, Gordly said she has "confidence that the changes... will be assigned the necessary and required urgency and oversight."

Workers joke about syndrome.

The anonymous letter referred to public remarks Gordly made during a statewide conference on diversity. At the conference, Gordly, D-Portland, introduced a Portland State University professor who had written a dissertation on post-traumatic slave syndrome.

The letter said a group of employees "seized on this statement and began a continual and drawn-out joke... stating that, in effect, black people are always making lame excuses for themselves and crying the blues."

An internal DHS report dated May 14 determined that a hospital employee, in fact, had learned about the theory of Post-Traumatic Slave Syndrome at the conference. The employee relayed the information to co-workers on Ward 48C, where Waters was a patient.

"Most of the people chuckled or

laughed, thinking it was absurd. No one took it seriously," the report quoted one mental health worker as saying. Another worker said, "We just thought it was ridiculous. "Another told investigators, "(I believe) there is stress related to being black, as well as being fat and other things."

Yet another mental health worker told investigators that during the discussion about Post-Traumatic Slave Syndrome, "(I recalled thinking)... I'm a Jew, and I'm not suffering from Post-Traumatic Nazi Syndrome. "The same employee, according to the report, had been chided by a supervisor for "unprofessional behavior" after writing in a nursing report that Waters and his black roommate were "birds of a feather."

Mazur-Hart admonished the comments of some of his employees.

"The discussion about Post-Traumatic Slave Syndrome on Ward 48C did not probe the meaningfulness of the criteria used in the concept, "he wrote in the DHs report. "Some of the staff challenged the concept in a sarcastic and abrupt way without attempting to evaluate its usefulness. "Even so, Mazur-Hart found there was "no compelling evidence of patient abuse in the form of racially harassing or discriminatory behavior."

DHS investigators also looked into a flier the anonymous letter claimed was circulated among the staff members mocking Waters, saying he suffered from "multi-ethnic post-past disorder."

The investigation confirmed the existence of "a handwritten document poking fun at a syndrome based only on ethnicity," Mazur-Hart wrote.

When asked by investigators about

the title, Multi-Ethnic Post-Past Disorder, an employee said, "Sounds familiar, but the title I wrote was something like Multi-Inherited Ethnic Stress Disorder."

Investigators allowed the employee to recreate the flier that the employee called "satire." Because the re-created flier did not target Waters or African Americans, Mazur-Hart determined there was no proof of patient abuse.

DHS "has taken, or is in the process of taking, personnel and management actions necessary to deal with the shortcomings that were uncovered, "Curtis said.

The new diagnosis is "appropriate."

The team also determined that a recent change in Water's psychiatric diagnosis, which caused him to be transferred from the hospital back to jail shortly after the investigation began, was "clinically appropriate and free from improper motivation."

Waters, who was diagnosed with paranoid schizophrenia by the hospital in the mid-1990s, was a patient from October 5, 2001, until March 21, when a state hospital doctor deemed him mentally capable to stand trial.

Waters was arrested on Sept. 17 after he allegedly aimed a pellet gun at police during a psychotic break, according to police and medical records. He is charged on the prosecutor's information with attempted aggravated murder, which may or may not stand when a grand jury ultimately considers Waters' mental condition and the fact he held a pellet gun.

Waters, Gordly's only child, was sent to the state hospital last fall—his third hospitalization there—after a judge determined that he was unable to aid in his defense. Waters was to receive treatment there to restore his fitness to go to trial or make other decisions about his case.

On March 21, about 10 days after the Justice Department's investigation began, records show, a hospital psychiatrist declared Waters able to aid and assist in his defense and changed his diagnosis from paranoid schizophrenia to paranoid personality disorder, a behavioral problem. Waters was taken back to the Justice Center Jail to face charges. Gordly and several authorities close to the case questioned the timing and results of Waters' new diagnosis.

The team found that Waters' diagnosis change was the result of long-standing physician disagreement over his symptoms. To that end, the team recommended the hospital implement a method by which "differences of opinion among physicians be resolved in a timely and effective manner."

Waters has had an issue since being moved from a jail cell back to the Oregon State Hospital's Portland facility, where he awaits another aid and assistance evaluation.

DOWN EVERY AVENUE, A DEAD END – Oregonian, The (Portland, OR) – June 3, 2002- page A01

June 3, 2002 | Oregonian, The (Portland, OR) | MICHELLE ROBERTS – The Oregonian | Page A01

Summary: Man languishes in gulf between inadequate mental health system and jail

"Let me tell it to you like this, "Tyrone Water says, getting agitated. "If Hardy Myers wants to wiretap my mother's phone, he has the power to snap his fingers once it's done. Why is it crazy or insane to believe that? "

It's 9 o'clock, Easter morning, in a non-contact visiting booth at the Justice Center jail in Portland. Grasping a greasy phone receiver, Tyrone stares fiercely through a glass divider and insists that Oregon's attorney general is stalking him.

Seven months ago, Tyrone's delusions placed him in the sights of a police revolver. Tyrone narrowly escaped death, and Oregon faced the controversy of a white officer killing the mentally ill son of its African American woman senator, Avel Gordly.

For more than a decade, Gordly watched her son struggle with his mental illness in a treatment system designed for and by whites. Now she watches him struggle in a system designed for criminals.

Tyrone was charged with attempted aggravated murder and attempted first-degree assault for pointing what appeared to be a gun at an officer on Sept. 17. Police later discovered it was a pellet gun.

A judge determined that Tyrone, 36, was not mentally competent to stand trial and ordered him, for the third time, to the Oregon State Hospital in Salem.

On March 4, an anonymous letter appeared in Gordly's mailbox that named a nurse, three mental health technicians, and a unit director who allegedly made repeated racist comments about Tyrone and other African Americans on Ward 48C, a high security forensics unit.

The allegation drew the attention of the highest levels of state government and sparked an investigation into minority patients's treatment at Oregon's psychiatric hospital.

Ten days after the injury began, on March 21, a hospital psychiatrist declared Tyrone able to aid and assist in his defense and changed his diagnosis from paranoid schizophrenia to paranoid personality disorder, a behavioral problem. Tyrone was promptly sent back to jail to face charges.

His mother wasn't the first or only one to be suspicious. Was the sudden diagnosis change an effort to ease scrutiny by getting Tyrone out of the hospital? If he's able to aid and assist, why is he still so delusional?

Through visiting booth glass smeared with red lip prints from another inmate's girlfriend, Tyrone says he can't wait to go to court so he can plead guilty and go to prison.

Tyrone, wearing Nyquil blue jail scrubs, isn't aware the Oregon Department of Justice is investigating his state hospital care. He rambles on about phone bugs and wiretaps, oblivious to the one conspiracy of which he might actually be a victim.

A Bible rests on an elephant-shaped coffee table, a well-worn list tucked into the book of Psalms.

Gordly sits on her couch and considers the piece of paper she keeps meaning to have laminated: The 10 Principles of Support by the National Alliance for the Mentally Ill.

We will see the individual first, not the illness.

"I think I do OK with that one," Gordly says.

We recognize that mental illnesses are brain disorders.

"That one, too."

WHEN RACE AND MENTAL ILLNESS COLLIDE- Oregonian, The (Portland, OR) – June 2, 2002 – page A01

June 2, 2002 | Oregonian, The (Portland, OR) | MICHELLE ROBERTS – The Oregonian | Page A01

Summary: As he chases his demons, a black man careens into a showdown with police

Tyrone Waters sees the police uniform and steps back. A peculiar look settles in his eyes.

"It's OK," Portland Police Cmdr. Derrick Foxworth says as he advances. "We're here to help you."

Tyrone isn't buying it.

The mentally ill son of Avel Gordly, Oregon's first African American woman senator, stopped taking his medications and grew convinced that government operatives were chasing him. For the past several weeks, he's ridden buses day and night, staying on the move and slipping deeper into the delusion.

Sirens shriek. Radios crackle. Officers surround, then hunker behind trees and telephone poles. This moment plays perpetually in Tyrone's mind.

Today, Sept. 17, it plays on North Williams Avenue.

"So it's going to be like this," an officer remembers Tyrone muttering as he pulled what appeared to be a pistol from his backpack. "So it's going to be like this."

At 36, Tyrone is the embodiment of one of the state's most pressing social dilemmas.

He lives on the fault line of the mental health system—a system that invests tens of millions of dollars a year in medications, counseling, and other services for the mentally ill but abandons them at the very moment their disease detonates: when the symptoms of their brain disorders make them dangerous to themselves and others.

Of the tens of thousands of Oregonians who pass through the system each year, many will tangle with police, adding to a nationwide truth: more mentally ill people are in jail than in psychiatric hospitals.

There are many stories such numbers do not tell. One is how much more difficult it is to beat those odds if you are a person of color.

Tyrone, one of the hundreds of thousands of African Americans estimated to have brain disorders in the United States, has intersected with police mostly because he won't use a mental health system that is built on white middle-class norms.

The prevalence of mental disorders is estimated to be higher among African Americans than whites because of stressors such as poverty and discrimination. Yet because of mistrust, stigma, cost, and clinician bias, it is much more difficult for them to receive appropriate treatment.

A mother possessing the power and influence of a senator can change a lot of things. Not that.

Angry black man. That, more or less, was Tyrone's first psychiatric diagnosis at age 24.

He'd just been fired from a job he'd held for two years, cleaning Delta passenger planes between flights.

Disappointed didn't cover it. An aviation career was Tyrone's castle in the air. He took hydraulics classes at Benson High School and trained as an aircraft mechanic during four honorable years in the U.S. Navy and dreamed of a steward position at Delta.

Gordly, a longtime Portland civil rights activist, didn't discourage her son's suspicion that his termination might have been discriminatory. The experience of folks in her world produced a saying: Last hired, first fired.

Then something swerved. Tyrone got another job working for a Boeing contractor in Hillsboro. But he spent his entire paycheck—thousands of dollars over several months—on an elaborate mail campaign, urging businesses from Corvallis to Tokyo to boycott Delta.

Gordly said she hopes the investigation will ultimately improve the "overall treatment climate for all patients, not just African Americans."

Investigators will also look into whether Water's psychiatric treatment was tainted by the alleged abuse. But because Mazur-Hart makes the ultimate ruling and is named in the letter, the attorney general's office will review it, said Curtis, who expects the review to be concluded by the end of the month.

Mazur-Hart welcomed the oversight. "We'll find out exactly what the status is as seen by someone outside the hospital," he said.

The Justice Department will also try to determine, based on the investigation results, whether management practices have "created a hostile work environment" in which employees have been threatened or retaliated against for trying to bring alleged problems to light, Curtis said.

Interviewed by phone Thursday, Waters said he was unaware of the situation described in the letter until investigators asked him about it.

However, he said he heard several other racist comments at the state hospital. Waters, who filed dozens of grievances, said one of the employees named in the letter once referred to him with a racial slur and said, "You're never going to make it out of here."

Waters said, "Nobody believed me until this employee had the guts to speak up about what was going on."

Waters was arrested on Sept. 17 after he allegedly aimed a pellet gun at police during a psychotic break, according to police and medical records. The police fired five live rounds and two beanbag rounds. Waters was hit with a beanbag round.

He is charged with attempted aggravated murder.

Gordly says her son was suicidal at the time of the shooting and had hoped to provoke police into killing him. She said he told her several times that he wanted to be with his father, who died a few years ago. Waters denies he was suicidal but admits being "distressed."

A question of mental fitness

Waters, Gordly's only child, was sent to the state hospital last fall—his third hospitalization there—after Multnomah County Circuit Judge Julie Frantz determined that he was unable to aid in his defense. Waters was to receive treatment there in an effort to restore his fitness to go to trial or make other decisions about his case.

State hospital doctors also make determinations about whether a mental disease or defect limits a person's criminal responsibility.

On March 21, about 10 days after the investigation began, records show, a hospital psychiatrist declared Waters able to aid and assist in his defense and changed his diagnosis from paranoid schizophrenia to paranoid personality disorder, a behavioral problem.

Waters was immediately transported back to the Multnomah County Justice Center Jail to face charges.

Gordly and several authorities close to the case have questioned the timing and results of Water's most recent evaluation, as well as the new diagnosis.

Curtis said Waters' evaluation was scheduled in accordance with time limits set by state law. But the matter is being investigated nonetheless, she said.

Mazur-Hart said he could not comment on Waters' specific situation but said, "The staff of this hospital do a remarkable job... dealing with these complicated issues on a regular, day-to-day basis. It's difficult work, and we have competent staff."

At a court appearance Thursday, Frantz ordered Waters to undergo another evaluation—not at the state hospital—after his attorney, Randall Vogt, said he was not convinced Waters was thinking clearly enough to make decisions about his case.

Waters repeated in court what he has said frequently: that he would rather go to prison for decades than go back to the state hospital.

"If that decision is based on delusional thinking or an unreasonable or irrational version of the facts, then I can't say for sure if he is able to aid and assist," Vogt told the judge.

The new evaluation will be completed within three weeks.

We will never give up hope.

She pauses.

"I need to work on that one," she finally admits, her proud son performing a magic trick at age 11 in a picture frame behind her. "I find myself always waiting for the other shoe to drop."

Gordly followed her frustration with Oregon's mental health system to advocacy. She sponsored legislation, testified, and lobbied for cultural competency in services she found lacking for all and failing people of color.

Despite years of effort, the anonymous letter brought an unfamiliar feeling of helplessness. "This can't be," Gordly remembers crying as she read it. "This can't be."

It crossed her mind that perhaps Tyrone had sent it. When his illness is in full force, he is prolific, sending threatening, though creative, letters to everyone from the FBI to the president. In January, Tyrone mailed Portland Police Chief Mark Kroeker, addressed to Mark KKK, a flier decorated with the help of the state hospital dayroom craft box: an origami paper hood with glitter glued in eye holes.

Gordly quickly dismissed the idea that this letter had come from Tyrone because it was typed and referred to public remarks she made during a statewide conference on diversity. Tyrone hadn't attended, but she remembered that several state hospital employees and managers had.

At the conference, Gordly introduced a Portland State University professor who had written a dissertation on post-traumatic slave syndrome. The letter said a group of employees "seized on this statement and began a continual drawn-out joke. They belittled you for making it. They belittled your son for believing it, and they belittled black people in general, stating that, in effect, black people are always making lame excuses for themselves and crying the blues."

And now, regardless of whether Tyrone's new diagnosis is collusion or coincidence, he is vulnerable.

On April 8, three days after Gordly comforts herself with NAMI affirmations, Tyrone's lawyer, Randall Vogt, raises concerns about his client's mental competency in court. Prosecutor Jim McIntyre, who received several of Tyrone's profane letters, including one that contained feces, doesn't object.

Gordly sighs relief when Multnomah County Circuit Judge Julie Frantz orders a second mental health evaluation for Tyrone, who responds angrily. He wants to go to prison.

"May I hug him? "Gordly asks the corrections deputy as he handcuffs her scowling son to take him back to jail.

"No," the deputy says. "Then I'd have to strip-search him. You wouldn't want that, would you? "

Gordly doesn't flinch. She'll save her anger until she's alone. She smiles at her son and tells him something she's trying to believe.

"It's going to be OK, Tyrone."

Three weeks later, Tyrone's new mental health evaluation is complete. Another Caucasian clinician, while acknowledging that Tyrone's symptoms rise and fall depending on the day, has found that he is ready for trial.

That, despite a frantic call from a jail employee to Gordly saying Tyrone is "deteriorating." That, despite word that Tyrone has been placed in an isolation cell for refusing to take his medications and calling a jail counselor a nasty name. Despite the drawings and the death threats, Tyrone continues to mail them to McIntyre and other public officials.

During a court hearing on April 29, Tyrone casts more doubt about whether he should be trusted with his future. He urgently begs Frantz to keep jail staff from tormenting him.

"I was served dinner by a female

blonde, white Multnomah County Sheriff's deputy in cell 5C-9 in lockdown. The meal consisted of chili, white rice, coleslaw, cake, and juice—Kool-Aid, if you will. The sheriff's officer gave me my meal with pubic hair and urine on it.

Gordly, divorced from Tyrone's father since he was 3, usually would have pulled up a chair and licked the envelopes. This was different. Her son was beyond disenchantment. Delta employees were following him; he confided in a timid whisper. He insisted they'd slashed his tires, although Gordly never saw damage.

Gordly was raised to shield signs of emotion and weakness from the white world. She wrestled with this impartation, then urged Tyrone to go to the Veterans Affairs Medical Center for a mental health evaluation.

Sociologists have studied what Gordly says happened next.

"They basically treated him like he had an attitude problem," she said. "Like he was a hostile, angry, black male. They told him to get over it and move on."

The hospital, citing confidentiality, declined to discuss the case. However, hospital officials said that since the mid-1990s—years after Tyrone's experience—they began requiring diversity and cultural competency training for staff and clinicians.

The Harvard University School of Public Health found in March that African Americans get poorer quality mental health care than whites.

Other research has shown broad racial inequities in medicine for decades, but the Harvard study was one of the first to show bias exists in mental health treatment regardless of socioeconomic status.

After work one day, Gordly slipped out of her heels, stepped on a screw, and discovered that Tyrone had removed the heat vents in the Northeast Portland apartment they shared. When she asked why, he looked incredulous.

Don't tell me you can't hear them, she remembers him saying.

Hear what?

The voices. The voices are coming from the ducts.

Gordly listened. Silence.

She frantically tried to find an African American psychiatrist. There is no such luck in a state where they can be counted on one hand.

Gordly urged Tyrone to try another hospital. He said he wouldn't listen to another white doctor tell him he was a thug.

Spend some time in Tyrone's life, and you will see why a young African American man—even one with educated, middle-class parents—might mistrust a mental health system that is the product of white, middle-class culture. The eyes that follow you through department stores, maybe. The brush-off: "Thank you for applying. We'll be in touch. "Or the scene that plays on your blocks as frequently as Starbucks builds in the burbs: your friends spread-eagled on the hoods of police cars.

One main consequence of a mental health system primarily geared to and run by whites is that African

Americans, in particular, tend to avoid treatment until the symptoms of their mental illnesses are severe, as national studies have shown.

For many, it means inpatient care, often at public expense. The Mental Health Law Project, based in Washington, D.C., published a study showing that African American men are admitted to county and state-funded psychiatric hospitals at a rate almost three times greater than white men and black women at a rate 2.5 times greater than white women.

The personal expense for Tyrone was far greater.

Months turned into four years. Tyrone tucked the minirecorders into the heating ducts. Gordly's hair turned gray. He cruised around town with a "Boycott Delta" sign taped in his rear window. She watched lines burrow permanently into her forehead. He complained that government officials had bugged their apartment. She became one.

"I know they're watching me," he'd say. "I love you" was all she could say.

Gordly lost count of the nights she dragged Tyrone into the emergency room when she feared he wanted to kill himself.

"On the 23rd of this month, the following comments were heard on the officer's radio in module 5-B: 'We got Waters dead.' 'We're not federal.' 'We want you dead, d-e-a-d. Dead.' 'We don't settle.'

The judge interrupts: "Did you state those were over a loudspeaker? "

"Over the officer's radio and the intercom system, "Tyrone replies earnestly.

Vogt calls Gordly to the stand.

"In order to move forward," Gordly tells Frantz. "We need to have an evaluation of my son by someone who is culturally competent... a mental health professional who comes with certain life experience, an understanding of what it is to live as an African American man in this society, and how that intersects with mental health issues."

Many have stopped her on the street and offered encouragement as a mother and support for the greater cause.

Some have accused her of pulling political strings from her son. Others have said Tyrone is dangerous and should go to prison. She has chosen her truth: This situation reflects more than her son's character, or lack thereof. It reflects a state's character, too.

"Again, my son is not a criminal," she testifies. "He has a mental illness. And he needs to be and deserves to be in a treatment setting."

She knows that if she presses, because of who she is, waiting lists can be circumvented, rules can be bent, and attention will be paid. Until this whole mess is resolved, Tyrone must go to another hospital. But where?

"Exactly what are the options available for my son and any other person in his circumstance? "Gordly asks the judge. "He can't go back to the Oregon State Hospital; I think we're all clear about that. That's a hostile environment for him."

The state hospital in Salem is the only place in Oregon designed to treat the mentally ill until they are well enough to face criminal charges, if ever.

"It is a very frustrating situation

in which this community finds itself, that there are not adequate options available for placements of individuals such as your son, "Frantz says. "Unfortunately, I don't have answers for you. I wish I did."

Whether Tyrone's situation can be blamed on a decade's worth of cultural incompetency isn't the issue the court must address.

Tyrone is enraged when the judge declares him unable to aid and assist, despite what the psychologist said. He understands the charges against him, but his delusions are too powerful to render him able to cooperate with his attorney.

On the way out of the courtroom, Tyrone won't look at his mother. He spits a mouthful of water on McIntyre's suitcoat.

Epilogue

On May 8, after discussing what she termed "the unique circumstances of this case" with Oregon State Hospital Supt. Stanley Mazur-Hart, Frantz ordered Tyrone to the hospital's Portland facility until he was well enough for trial. Because the hospital's only forensics ward is in Salem, the state is paying for two hospital employees to monitor Tyrone individually.

Gordly is relieved that her son is back in a hospital setting, although she continues to doubt the cultural competency of his care. She visits him frequently and prays.

Tyrone has good days and bad. Last week, he got in trouble for spitting grape juice at other patients and threatening to kill Mazur-Hart. His anti-psychotic medication has recently been increased by a third.

The Oregon Department of Justice continues to investigate whether management practices at the hospital have led to racial harassment, discrimination, and other civil rights violations inside the state's largest psychiatric facility. Mazur-Hart has declined to discuss the investigation except to say that "we just need to see what the review presents. If there is any merit to the allegations, then he would need to work on getting those things fixed.

The results are expected this week.

Call it the failure of a white mental health system to understand a black man. Call it Tyrone's inability or unwillingness to seek help. It doesn't matter. Nobody but his mother lamented the disconnect until Tyrone's problem became society's. That is, the day he tried to set fire to the Justice Center.

On Nov. 22, 1994, black Voit sneakers powdered a black man with a braid toward an occupied corrections van at Northeast Sixth Avenue and Killingsworth Court, where he sloshed gasoline and tossed a lighted book of matches, which failed to ignite.

Ten minutes later, Tyrone wedged his 1972 Cadillac Fleetwood into a 10-minute parking zone outside the Justice Center.

He trailed the rest of the five-gallon gas can around the 15-story jail engraved with the words of Martin Luther King Jr.: "Injustice anywhere is a threat to justice everywhere."

His preoccupation had passed from Delta to another perceived adversary: the police.

Tyrone was jailed for three months on charges of attempted arson after a judge told him, in front of his mother, that he was spoiled. After a court-appointed psychiatrist found him mentally ill to face trial, the judge sent him to the forensics ward at Oregon State Hospital in Salem on February 9, 1995.

But three months later, he was sent back to jail, where two months in the isolation of a jail cell took their toll. A judge ordered him to go back to the hospital. Three months later, an explanation—besides his character—was proffered: paranoid schizophrenia.

This validation didn't erase Tyrone's distrust of mental health professionals. But when told he wasn't to blame for his brain disorder, he agreed to treatment.

He swallowed anti-psychotic pills

handed to him in small white ketchups, but the side effects were excruciating. On a scale of one to ten, the muscle pain "was a twenty." Tyrone's jaw twisted and locked. His walk was stilted and jerky, he said, like he was trying to moonwalk forward.

Before long, Tyrone was released on probation with the requirement that he continue treatment.

Determined to keep her son from becoming a digit in the disturbing data set of black men behind bars, Gordly searched for a private doctor. If not an African American, at least someone who understood her son's culture.

Dr. Charles Bellville, a soft-spoken psychiatrist who was raised in the South, came highly recommended by a family friend. Bellville, young and Caucasian, asked Tyrone if he "felt comfortable working with a white man. "Just the question put Tyrone at ease. He melted into Bellville's vintage sofa.

Unlike other fields of medicine, where laboratory tests can aid in diagnosis, psychiatry relies on symptoms and signs as witnessed.

Research has found that African American men are twice as likely as white men to be diagnosed with paranoid schizophrenia. Such misdiagnosis is often based on cultural insensitivity because whites frequently misperceive black men as paranoid and volatile, according to a 1999 report by the U.S. Surgeon General.

Nationally, African American patients also tend to be concentrated at state hospitals, where understaffing and poor patient management practices also contribute to misdiagnosis.

Bellville didn't discount Tyrone's schizophrenic diagnosis. But he didn't focus on it either.

"My basic goal with Tyrone was to establish trust so we could try medications," Bellville said.

Three years ago, the U.S. surgeon general published research showing that a third of African Americans are slow metabolizers of several antipsychotic medications and, consequently, easier to overmedicate and more prone to side effects.

So Bellville tried Tyrone on the latest medications at low doses, increasing them slowly as needed. When Tyrone, who was already on $600 a month in Social Security disability payments, came up short at the pharmacy, Bellville gave him free samples.

The medications did not erase Tyrone's paranoia, but they helped. Bellville spent hours helping Tyrone understand that, even if he believed something, he could keep from obsessing over it.

Even so, Belllville never wrote off Tyrone's delusions as simple insanity. The content of hallucinations and delusions often reflects personal experience. "Every pearl starts with a grain of sand, "Bellville said, particularly of Tyrone's suspicion of police.

Months turned into four years. Tyrone worked as a live-in caregiver for his grandfather and completed computer courses at Portland Community College's skills center. A neatly framed certificate on his dresser gave him an unfamiliar jolt of confidence.

Mother and son reserved Sunday mornings for each other. They ordered breakfast takeout and ate over laughter at Gordly's dining room table. Then they swayed to gospel CDs or watched "Meet the Press."

How long had it been since Gordly felt close to her son—close to the person without the intrusion of his illness? How long would it last?

"Don't worry," Tyrone told her. "I'm going to make it."

"Ten. . .nine. . . eight. . .seven. . . six. . ." Tyrone counted down in staccato on his mother's answering machine. "Five. . . four. . . three. . . two. . ."

On Sept. 17, Gordly punched rewind and sent her son's foreboding message squiggling in reverse. She didn't know what it meant, but the possibilities haunted her.

This chapter of Tyrone's life started

in 1999, when he fell into a common trap. Mistaking his clearer thinking for recovery. Tyrone decided to forgo the $700-a-month prescription hassle. He promptly grew paranoid and stopped seeing Bellville.

Gordly and her siblings decided Tyrone couldn't care for his grandfather anymore. They helped him move into an apartment, where he immediately accused a property manager of sneaking into his studio and urinating in his food.

As Tyrone headed back into the shadows of his illness, something happened that robbed Gordly of sleep for months.

On April 1, 2001, Jose Santos Victor Mmejia Poot, a 29-year-old Mexican national, was shot in the head and chest after he charged Portland police with a rod he pulled from the door of a private psychiatric hospital where he was a patient.

The shooting outraged community groups, and their anguish amplified when a Multnomah County grand jury cleared the officers of criminal wrongdoing and Police Chief Mark Kroeker defended his department's shoot-to-kill policy.

On May 5, Cinco de Mayo, Gordly served as a liaison between police and more than 1,000 marchers who streamed through downtown protesting Mejia's killing. As hundreds cheered for the end of what they called racist social policies, her worries were more personal.

Two weeks after Mejia died, Tyrone snarled to his neighbor, "Someone could shoot you through these walls." Tyrone wasn't home when the police came, so his landlord let them in. His illness was palpable in the single can of food in the cupboards and the locked safe in the freezer.

Evicted in August, Tyrone moved into a motor home parked in his grandfather's backyard. He wasn't there much. Convinced that government types were following, he rode buses nonstop, trying to shake them.

Gordly could reach him only on his cellphone, and even that was hit and miss. Tyrone often decided the feds had discovered his frequency, and we're tracking him. Each time, he tossed his phone into the river and replaced it at Radio Shack.

One afternoon, Tyrone, described as a "crazed passenger," tried to stop a Tri-Met bus near Jantzen Beach. The police searched his briefcase and found a BB gun designed to look like a semi-automatic pistol. Officers arrested him for unlawfully carrying a firearm and took him to jail. "I'm going to kill Hardy Myers, "Tyrone pledged from the back seat a few hours before he was released.

And then, a couple of weeks later, Tyrone counted down ominously on his mother's answering machine.

Gordly dialed the only person she trusted with his problem. Maybe Tyrone wouldn't be so frightened and so volatile if a black officer approached him, she told her friend, Derrick Foxworth, the police commander.

Foxworth was concerned about his friend's son as well as his officers. They're the ones who pick up the slack for the mental health system, he frequently grumbled. They're the ones who get blamed when things go bad.

A week earlier, on Sept. 11, a manager from the Meier & Frank collections department called 9-1-1 to report a disturbing message she'd heard on Tyrone's voice mail while trying to exact the $200 he owed for Freedom by Tommy Hilfiger cologne products.

"I want you. . . dead," Tyrone recorded himself saying. "You will be involved in a shootout on the day you attempt to take me into custody."

Ever since, fliers with Tyrone's scowling mug shot hung on precinct bulletin boards that said: Tyrone is out in the community. There's no warrant for his arrest, so approach him cautiously. He's mentally ill, and he doesn't trust the police. Foxworth didn't have to spell it out. Everyone knows what the flier's for: We don't want another Mejia.

After Tyrone's phone threat, Foxworth assigned a detective to find Tyrone, hoping they could catch him off-guard on the street and get him safely to a hospital for a mental evaluation. Six unsuccessful days later, the notion made Foxworth chuckle. Tyrone off-guard. Fat chance.

But at 6:30 p.m. on Sept. 17, they knew where he was. "He's at my dad's house on North Williams Avenue," Gordly had said. "I'm afraid."

Foxworth called to the next glass cubicle for Lt. Kevin Modica, who is also African American.

They decided to go themselves. If things went bad, they didn't want an officer to read his name on a protest banner for doing what he was trained to do. If things went bad, it would be better for the bureau—and less divisive for the city—if it wasn't on the back of a white officer.

"It's OK," Foxworth tells Tyrone

as he advances. "We're here to help you."

Tyrone freezes, pulls what looks like a gun from his backpack, and raises it. A phrase sticks in Foxworth's head: suicide by police. Gordly had told him that Tyrone had talked about wanting to be with his father, a retired U.S. Army Corps of Engineers captain who died that month a few years earlier.

Modica radios for cover and a beanbag gun, or less-lethal, they call it. Foxworth negotiates. Sirens shriek. Radios crackle. Officers surround, then hunker behind trees and telephone poles.

Tyrone won't drop the gun but flinches when an officer strikes him with a beanbag round. Then five live rounds—fired by a white officer who arrived not knowing the delicate dynamic—crack the evening air.

"No, no, no!" Less lethal only! "An officer hears Modica yell as Tyrone falls face forward.

Heaven help us! Foxworth remembers praying silently. We've shot the mentally ill son of Oregon's first African American woman senator.

Moments later, Gordly sprints toward a ribbon of yellow police tape. She breaks through in time to see her son hoisted onto a stretcher.

Foxworth yanks her into his arms before she can scream. Tyrone is alive, he assures. An officer fired five shots and missed.

But when the paperwork is done, the senator's son faces finality of another sort: decades in prison for the attempted aggravated murder of a police officer.

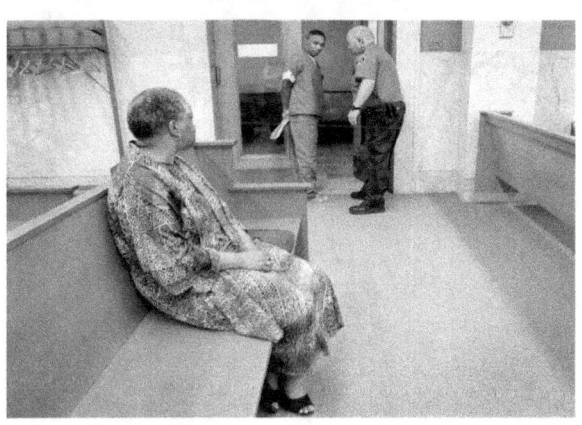

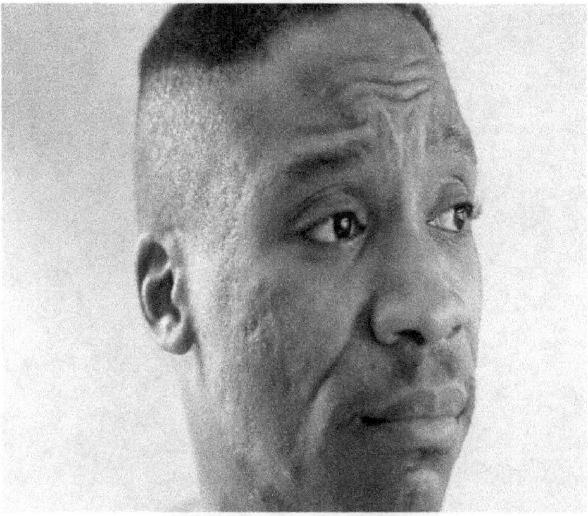

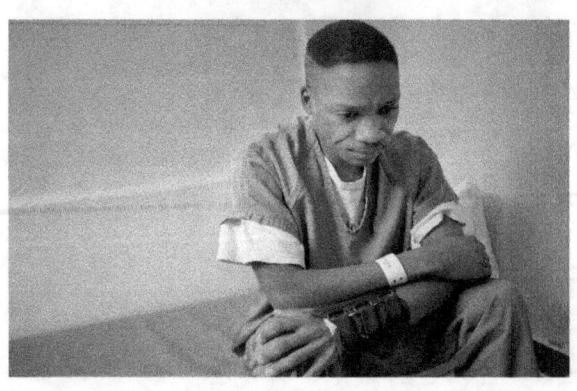

For God so loved the world that He gave His only begotten Son, that whoever believes in Him should not perish but have everlasting life.

-John 3:16, NKJV

That if you confess with your mouth the Lord Jesus and believe in your heart that God has raised Him from the dead, you will be saved.

-Romans 10:9, NKJV